THE SECOND LANE OF A TWO-WAY STREET

A Journey on the
Value of Friendship and Unconditional Love

Traci Engle

The Second Lane of a Two-Way Street
Copyright © 2018 by TEngle Consulting Group, Inc.

Authored by Traci Engle

ISBN 978-1-7321086-0-8

Printed in USA

Just don't wait for someone or something to shake up your snow globe!

-Traci

***

I dedicate this very personal recount of my *Journey* to Mom and Dad. May the moments captured in these pages remind you of the strength and courage you have instilled in me.

* * *

Table of Contents

Introduction

My friends have been asking me why I took the time to write a book. You see, writing is not something that was ever a passion. The Journey of 2017 made me realize how blessed I was. I wanted to share the tips, tidbits and lessons I learned along the way. I wanted you, the reader, to know you are not alone. My challenge was cancer. However, this book and lessons within apply to life. How we look at each day and how we face our demons is in some respects a choice. Life can be difficult. Gosh if it were easy…now wouldn't that be boring? ☺ Sometime our 'snow globe of life' is shaken… sometimes it shakes a bit too much. May this book be something you can turn to knowing you are not alone.

CHAPTER 1

Living My Dream Life

I t was 2017, and at 47 years old, I had what I thought was a perfect life. I was living in one of the most prestigious neighborhoods in the Bay Area. I was running a successful consulting firm that I started from nothing. I was living the American Dream.

Mind you, I got here on my own based on years of hard work and discipline to save financially. I felt accomplished. I loved my life. Yes, it was crazy busy. But I was happy; or so I thought. Days were jam packed ensuring clients and consultants were happy. The days were long, and although I tried to fit in exercise, it sometimes felt like I was just going through the motions. I was shocked to learn you are supposed to sweat when you work out! I was so tired after work, I was lucky to be at the gym. Lately, my favorite exercise was meditation yoga where you just sat, meditated and on occasion, fell asleep. Heaven!

My typical day was... wake up at 6:00am, check and respond to emails, watch the stock market (while dreaming of retirement), get ready, and plow through my day of meetings. I ended the day with a quick workout, late dinner and in bed by 10:00pm. Somehow, I managed to fit nights out with friends during the week. On weekends, I tried to catch up but mostly found myself napping.

Then, with just one phone call, my life was forever changed.

The day after my routine mammogram appointment, I received a call from the doctor's office informing me I needed to make an appointment for a follow up image and possible ultrasound. The only facilities that had the equipment necessary for the tests were in Fremont or Palo Alto.

"What? That is not going to work," I said. That would require me to take a lot of time off work and would impact my clients. You see, those two locations were over an hour drive each way. "Couldn't we just retake the images at the Danville imaging center?" A location that was a ten-minute drive from my house.

Then I said, "You know, before I jump the gun and rush in, can the doctor call me?"

I mean, seriously, is this a fuzzy film? Or is there something of concern? I just wanted answers before I started rearranging my schedule.

My messages and questions got routed to three different people, and three different people from three different departments called me. (Mind you, none of these calls were from my doctor.) Of course, I got three different responses! UGH!

So, I said, "Okay, just book the first available appointment. Let's just get this over with."

The follow up visit was booked for Monday, March 20.

I arrived early. I had never been to this medical facility before. It was fairly new. I was impressed. I waited patiently in the lobby until they called my name. Of course, during my wait I was on email responding to clients.

Then my name was called. The technician started to take the mammogram when I started asking her questions.

"It was probably just a fuzzy film, right?"

She responded, "Honey, with today's technology we really don't get fuzzy films anymore."

4

"Oh," I said.

After the imaging, she said they would let me know the results. I said, "GREAT!" I got out my phone and pulled up my calendar. "When can I expect them?"

She said, "In five minutes."

My first thought was, "Now that is what I call service!"

Why couldn't all test results be ready so quickly? It would save a lot of unnecessary time waiting. I sat patiently as I continued to respond to emails.

She came back in and said, "Okay. The imaging does show a mass and we need to get an ultrasound."

"Great," I said. "When can we schedule it?"

She said, "Now. They are waiting for you across the hall."

A different technician greeted me and performed the ultrasound. When it was completed, the technician said they would let me know the results.

"GREAT," I said. "When can I expect them?"

She said, "In five minutes." This time when I was hit with this quick response, I started to get worried. I have had ultrasounds before and results typically needed someone special to read them. Hmm... I decided not to worry and continued to pass the time responding to work emails.

She came back in and said, "Okay. You now need a biopsy to determine what the mass is."

"Great," I said. "When can we schedule this?"

5

She said, "Now. The radiologist will be with you in five to ten minutes."

Now, mind you, it was 10:40am at this point. Any of you that know me, know that I like to optimize my day. How can I get the most things done in a short period of time? This appointment was just the start of my day. So, if I was going to be in Palo Alto, I was going to drive home through Foster City to see friends and clients. I had the whole day planned!

I told her, "Wait... you don't understand. At 11:00am, I have a conference call to facilitate a vender demo. I need to log into the call. And I have a 12:30pm lunch appointment and two coffee appointments this afternoon. Just how long will this take?"

She just looked at me and said, "We can give you a few minutes to cancel and rearrange your meetings."

Apparently, I wasn't going to be able to make the demo conference call. I asked if I would still be able to make my lunch appointment.

She just looked at me and calmly said, "Maybe, but you probably won't want to."

I did not really understand that last part "you probably won't want to." These are clients. Of course, I want to see them. So, I hopped on my phone and cancelled my 11:00am and 12:30pm meetings but kept my coffee appointments.

They completed the biopsy. I had no idea what to expect. The biopsy was a scary procedure. The tool used made loud noises and when completed, the area was swollen and sore. They gave me a mini ice pack. Seriously? An ice pack for the boob? Whoa! I started to get scared. I asked when I could expect results. This time I was hit with the typical response I was used to. You should know results in one to two days. Figures. The most important result and they make you wait. Now, I thought that was cruel!

After I was dressed and packing up to leave, the technician asked if I had a surgeon. WHAT? Excuse me? Now wait. I just came in for pictures. I can take a card or your recommendation. But really, I am not sure I need it.

She gave me a card.

I got to my car. I sat for a second to absorb what had just happened this morning and I started to cry uncontrollably.

I went in for follow up pictures. When I told my friends prior to this day they all responded, "Oh, that is common. Breast tissue can be fibrous, and they often need extra films." That comforted me some. But in my car sobbing, I now needed to pull myself together. For gosh sake, I have client coffee meetings in a few hours.

I did make it to my coffee meetings in Foster City. Although, my mind wandered, and I became more concerned as the day progressed. I was sure it was nothing, but now I wanted those results. Why did those results take more than five minutes? In just a few hours I went from sobbing to totally freaking out!

My last coffee appointment was over. It was 5:00pm, and I was headed home during rush hour traffic. This didn't bother me as sitting in silence during my drive would help me get a grip on the day. I pulled out of my client's parking lot and proceeded to merge with traffic onto the bridge. A sigh of relief. I made it through my client meetings without too much emotion. Now I was on the bridge with at least an hour drive ahead.

Bumper-to-bumper traffic. I happened to glance at the car right next to me. The driver was a very attractive woman who had no hair. I am not talking old with thinning hair. She obviously was undergoing chemotherapy treatment for cancer. She had on makeup and was beautiful; but bald. Bald like the *Saturday Night Live* skit "The Skinheads." At that moment, I got a pit in my stomach. I knew that was God's way of preparing me for the news. I continued to cry uncontrollably.

7

That night I didn't get any sleep.

I went to work the next day and waited for the phone to ring. Literally. I called my cell from the desk phone. Yep, it is working. I took my phone with me to every meeting. That phone and I were glued at the hip. 2:00pm. No phone call. Is this good or bad?

Hmmm… I decide to call the doctor. The nurse said, "Oh. Your doctor is out of the office for a week."

WHAT?!?! I need those results now! I mean, seriously. Yesterday the results were released to me in five minutes. Now I must wait a week? No way!

She said, "Oh. I do see the results are in and there is a message for the doctor to call you. I will route it to the doctor on call."

Whew… now I should hear soon!

3:00pm. No call. 3:15pm. No call. 3:30pm. The phone rings. It is my primary care doctor asking if anyone had called me.

I say, "No, but so glad you called Doc! I just need my results, so I can sleep tonight. Can you read them to me?" (Apparently, results must be delivered by a doctor.)

She said, "Where are you right now? Are you close to the medical offices?"

"What? Why? What's up Doc… just give it to me straight."

She paused, "I am sorry, Traci. The results came back positive. You have cancer."

Those words lingered… *you… have… cancer*.

I am not sure I remember much more of the conversation. I was at my client's office. I walked to the kitchen area and just sat in the back listening. Listening to the findings, listening to next steps…

The part I did remember was my doctor asking, "Do you want me to prescribe something to help you sleep?"

For the first time in my life I said, "Yes. Please!"

And that is one day in my life I won't forget... March 21st.... 3:30pm. That is when I got the call that shook up my snow globe (aka my life).

What next? I needed to call my parents. How do you tell your parents you have cancer? I mean, at 47 years old I was supposed to be the one taking care of my parents; not the other way around.

My family is over 3,000 miles away in Ohio. It is at times like this that you need your family and friends.

That first night, I experienced my first panic attack. Have you ever had one? You would know if you did. They are not fun. I was in a light sleep and then my heart starting racing. I jumped out of bed pacing and crying uncontrollably. I tried to talk myself out of it.

"Breathe!!!" I kept telling myself.

When you are given a diagnosis of cancer, you rethink your life almost instantaneously. It is quite amazing how 47 years of life experiences flash before your eyes.

It is also interesting who you want to seek for comfort. Of course, there is family and close friends. But what about your ex-boyfriend? The one you haven't really spoken with in over a year. The one that knows you and has similar views on life. The one that you still carry with you even though you are not together. Do you call? What do you say? How do you broach this? No time to think. You are in the middle of a panic attack and you know he is the only one that can talk you off the ledge.

It is 11:40pm. I text, "Can you talk?"

9

I don't wait for a response. I then just call. He answers. (For this book, I will call him Travis.)

"Travis! It is me... I have cancer! Help what do I do?" (Mind you, this is all while I'm sobbing uncontrollably.)

Travis remains calm (as I knew he would). He says, "Stop... tell me again?"

I said, "I have cancer. I was diagnosed today with breast cancer. What am I going to do?"

Travis is at work. He works as a night supervisor for a large package distribution company. He is at his job, but he took my call and now is attempting to calm me down!

"Traci, breathe. You are going to be Okay! Breast cancer is the most common cancer in this area. If you are going to get anything, you are in the best area in the world to get breast cancer. You have Stanford, UCSF and other research areas. Marin county is known for the highest occurrence of breast cancer. You need to first just get all the facts."

I started to calm down. I actually smiled on the inside with that last comment. *You need to first get all the facts.* Yes! Travis was right! That is what I do all the time. Don't panic. Get the facts! Breathe. Breathe again! Sounds simple, but not so much tonight. After about 15 minutes, I was calmed down and Travis said he would check in tomorrow. (He did have to get back to his job.)

I should 'try' to get some sleep. I needed all the rest I could get to muster up strength and energy to tackle what was coming.

The next few days were a blur. The oncology department called at 4:20pm and scheduled me for an appointment with the oncology nurse for the next day. Then more appointments with surgeons...more tests including an MRI, 7 vials of blood, x-rays...

Thank goodness for my friends Annalisa, Patty and Lisa who were able to take off work and accompany me to my appointments! I really didn't remember anything I was told. They had to remind me of facts over the next week. Wait… March 21 was only two and a half days ago! It felt like an eternity!!!

For the first time in my life, I didn't ask when in the future I could fit in appointments. Instead, I informed my clients of my news and told them health was first and that I would need dedicated time off to focus 100% on my health. In fact, when the doctor offices would tell me the earliest they could fit me in was next week, I responded with, "That won't work. Can you take me today? I need to get in sooner!" Such a change in dialogue from just a few days ago!

The receptionists typically just looked at me. I told them, "I am serious. I am 100% dedicated to getting through all the doctor appointments and tests as soon as possible. I need the facts. This is cancer and not the flu. I want it OUT. ASAP!"

So, they worked together and got everything scheduled across 3 days.

Surgery was scheduled for April 20th at the Menlo Park Surgical Hospital. I would have a one to two-night stay, and then home care. Mom and Dad were coming out and my sister planned to join us on May 6.

Surgery was literally one month from the date of diagnosis. I just wanted to get the growth out as soon as possible. Cancer is never good, and I know from family history that cancer left untreated only gets worse and harder to combat. At the time of diagnosis, I was at Stage One. The pathology post-surgery classified it Stage Two. That was just in four weeks! My advice to all is don't wait or prolong the inevitable when it comes to diseases.

CHAPTER 2

Lesson 1 Realizing I Am Not Perfect

S o, why did I title this book *The Second Lane of a Two-Way Street*? Why not *My Journey Through the Unimaginable*? Good question.

You see, Cancer Treatment is a Journey. A journey unique to the individual. No two cancer patients will relate their experiences in exactly the same way. You see, we are all in different places in our lives. We all have a different past and a different future. Every experience we have lived is one only we can draw upon. Every experience we have lived could be one we have to relive if the life message is not learned.

If we go back to pre-diagnosis, my life was perfect. I was living the American Dream. I was living the lifestyle I wanted. I had great friends and family.

My neighbors, Betsy and Adam, would arrange backyard BBQs and Wine Nights. Sometimes we celebrated Champagne Sundays or Mimosa Mondays.

However, other than a few impromptu events with friends, I was just a bit too busy to really enjoy spending time with them. After all, the American Dream is working hard and making money to afford the things that make you happy. Right?

13

Vacation? What was that? I vaguely remember taking a vacation. I used to go to Paris every year. Can I still make that claim-to-fame if my last trip was twelve years ago?

All my friends would say I am the most loyal, dedicated friend they had. I mean, if anyone needed something I was there; day or night! No questions asked. My friends and family could count on me! I was the best friend anyone could ever have. I would always be there no matter what!

When they would ask what they could do for me, my typical response was, "I am good. I don't need anything." This was true. I didn't need anything. I had everything I needed and if I didn't, I could simply pay someone or buy something. I was a pillar... not needing to rely on others.

The Journey through Cancer Treatment taught me friendship is a two-way street. The only way friendship works is if you are *both* there for each other. Friends allow the other person to see you in less than perfect light. Friends know they will be there for you and that neither will judge.

Friendship for me was a one-way street. I was there for everyone! I didn't need anything... until now. Now my world was upside down and the journey I was about to embark upon required me to rethink everything down to the very essence of my core being. I found myself lost, confused and scared. Where do I start? How do I continue to be strong and yet be open to really experiencing and learning from this journey that was laid out for me?

My first stop was God. Yes, God. I called the church and made an appointment with the priest. Mind you, although I joined the local Catholic Church three years ago, I was more a C&E (Christmas and Easter) Catholic at this point in my life. But I had a feeling this journey was going to be one like no other, and it might not hurt to have some heavenly intervention. Really, I needed to come clean with God.

I had to take a hard look at myself. Was I really the person I wanted to be? I mean, I was a good person. Right? I didn't always go to church because I was too tired to get up on Sunday mornings. But I did good things for people. I belonged to the local Rotary Club and always found time to give back with either time or money. Didn't that count with God? But now faced with a life illness, I had to really look at my life. Did I always act in a God-like manor? Was there anything that I did that maybe wasn't so "angelic"?

The answers may shock my friends. Yes, there are things I had done over the years that I am not proud of. Things that go against the very core of who I am. I can just hear the thought going through your head, "Then why did you do those things if they were against your very core?" Good question.

I have realized that trying to explain the "why" only results in trying to justify the undesirable actions. There really is no good enough reason that would justify these actions. They happened. I am not proud of them. And to be honest, I knew that when they were happening. I just didn't see any consequence at the time and thought, "Who cares?" Well, now I cared. Now I needed to come clean with God. I needed to ensure that if I wasn't successful battling this cancer journey that at least I knew I was at peace with my God.

It is uncomfortable to be one-on-one with your priest. (It is actually worse than explaining to your parents that you wrecked the car!) You are sitting across from the "holy liaison" to God. You must tell the truth because God knows if you didn't.

So, I started, "Father, I am here to confess my sins." I paused. I took a deep breath and asked, "Just how much detail do you need? I mean, can I just summarize in cliff-note style or do you need a play-by-play?"

The Priest just smiled and said, "Tell me in your words."

So, I opted for the summarized version. He did the priestly thing, and I received my penance. I felt relieved. A huge weight was lifted. Why did I wait so long to go to confession? Oh yeah, I was busy running a business, living my dream life, and was invincible. Oh yeah, I now have cancer and realize I am not invincible.

———— CHAPTER THREE

Lesson 2
Forced to Ask
for Help

A sking for help seems so simple. People do it every day. "Hey, can you pick up my print out at the copier?"

"Can you review this document before I turn it in to my boss?"

"Hey, can you review this email before I send it? I don't want it to be mis-interpreted?".

Now, I found myself in a predicament. The life I had created was one alone. I felt almost like the "Grinch." Not that I was mean, of course not! I just lived alone. My life was self-sustaining. I liked it that way… until now. Now, I needed help. Not just a little bit of help. We are talking full on support and help on many levels were going to be needed for the foreseeable future. Who knows what lies ahead?

The thoughts going through my mind were:

* How was I going to survive financially? I am self-employed. I had wanted to hire back-office staff to assist with the operations, but I never got around to it. The company was run by one person... me. Would my business suffer? Or worse yet, would it cease to operate?

* How was I going to get to and from doctor appointments? I could drive myself, but they do suggest that you bring a friend. When you are diagnosed with a severe disease, your brain hears every third word. You just are on information overload. Friends can take notes...

* How quickly would I recover from surgery? I would need 24x7 care for a few weeks. How was that going to work?

* What if I needed chemotherapy? Or radiation? What care would I need?

* I have a cat, Bordeaux. Would I be able to take care of him?

You get the jest. Floods of questions flowing through my head. All "What ifs." All draining. All draining because I didn't have the answers. For once in my life, I couldn't plan the future. For once in my life, I had to live in the NOW and just let life unfold. (I just read what I wrote. "For once in my life I couldn't plan the future." Let's save this thought for Lesson 4. Now back to learning to ask for help.)

So, diagnosed on a Tuesday and my first oncology appointment was the next morning. I called my friend Patty. "Hi, Patty. Sorry to have to ask, but you know how I told you earlier today I was diagnosed with cancer? Well, my first oncology appointment is tomorrow; tomorrow afternoon. I can drive to and from. I know you are working and don't want to interfere with your job, but can you go with me? I think they have wi-fi, so you can work at the doctor office. I just need someone to be there with me. They say I won't remember the conversations and that I may not remember to ask questions. I will need someone to take notes so I can read later what they said. If you can't go with me, I totally understand. I mean it is such short notice?"

Whew... that was a lot! I think I spewed all that out without taking a breath. I sat silently and just prayed she could go with me. The response was quick, "Of course! What time do we need to leave?"

I sighed a HUGE sigh, gave her the time, and we hung up. Just Patty saying, "Of course! What time do I need to be ready?" was a huge relief. Asking for help was something I never did....

This asking for help continued as I relied on Lisa and Annalisa to take me to other doctor appointments. Some of these visits morphed into visits to labs, x-rays, etc. Not once did my friends waver. They allowed the day to unfold and stayed with me until the appointments were over. It was such a blessing to get all the doctor visits and tests done quickly. It allowed me to get all the facts quickly, so I could determine next steps.

Cancer treatment is long. It included surgery, chemotherapy and then reconstructive surgery. Start-to-finish, it spanned from March 20 to December 22; nine months.

For the surgery, my parents flew out and stayed with me for four weeks. My sister came out on the last week and also assisted. Asking for help was no longer confined to doctor visits. Now home from surgery, I needed help with everyday life - laundry, feeding Bordeaux, getting dressed, and (not to mention) house and yard work. Every spring, I would put down fresh mulch, check the irrigation system, fix any issues and then plant flowers and my vegetable garden. This year, I had to see if my dad and sis would help me with that. Otherwise, I would just have to live with my yard the way it was. My dad and sis wanted my yard to be perfect

THE SECOND LANE OF A TWO-WAY STREET

and beautiful so that I had someplace nice to sit out when I wasn't able to get out of the house. Mom took care of the inside - mopping, doing laundry, preparing food for all of us (including Bordeaux), and helping me with personal grooming. That last one was humbling. Seriously, being 47 years old and needing your mom to dress you? Very humbling!

I found that the more people I told that I had cancer, the more people volunteered to help! It was overwhelming how much support I received. My entire Rotary Club volunteered to help with meals. A different person brought meals every day post-surgery. Sometimes, they stayed and ate the meal with us which was nice to get company! With so much support, at times I just wanted the company and not the food. Going from being up and busy for 16 hours a day to recovering from surgery and being home 24x7, took a toll mentally. I found myself wanting to talk to friends via the phone. You may laugh. I mean, how else would you talk with friends? But in today's day and age, we text. Calling is a thing of the past. And with my friends all working and busy with their own lives, when was there time to talk? The only person who now had an infinite amount of free time was me! Hmm... what lesson was I supposed to get from all this down-time?

Chemotherapy went on for five months and often was weekly. I was not allowed to drive myself. This required 20 rides over the course of five months. I just want to give you a flavor of how much help I needed. Going from never asking for anything to asking for rides and company during chemo appointments was tough.

The toughest request for help came after my fourth chemo injection. The first four were the worst and very hard core. After the fourth chemo injection, I was so sick. I could not move from the couch for a full seven days... not even to sit up. I got up only to feed the cat and to heat up food for myself. During that time, friends reached out to see if I needed food. I just cried. I didn't need food. I was

20

able to heat up the left-overs Mom left for me, but now my kitchen sink was disgusting. Dishes were piled high. I'm sure the bottom dishes were growing mold or something. Worst yet, my kitchen smelled!! But I was so sick and weak, I couldn't do anything about it.

My neighbor Betsy texted, "Do you need food?"

Still crying, I texted back, "No, thank you for the offer!"

Then, I did it. I mustered up the strength to ask, "Hey, Betsy. I do need help with one thing."

She said, "Just name it!"

I responded, "I need help cleaning my kitchen. I am too weak and today is trash day."

She came over immediately and with no questions or judgements, emptied the dishwasher and reloaded the mess that was in the sink. I was never so embarrassed yet grateful. Forever grateful!

These forever grateful moments came quite often. With Cancer Treatment, you are at the mercy of friends and family. You can't do stuff. You just can't. It isn't optional. Rides to chemotherapy, personal care after surgeries, food and help as the body recuperates from treatment... all of this, you can't do it alone. I had to ask for help. Even asking for friends and my neighbors to just hang out and talk with me about anything... except cancer. My neighbors Adam and Betsy were always there; even last minute. They would prepare a mini party with appetizers and beverages. I drank my club soda. (Well, sometimes I had wine when it didn't make me nauseous.) These moments helped me feel normal.

Travis was also there a lot for me during this time. He would make homemade soup and Jell-O and drop it off. It meant a lot! One time, I asked, "Hey, can you make me Jell-O?" At the time I asked, I was on the easier Chemotherapy drugs and physically doing okay. I was not sick and still able to take care of myself.

He jokingly said, "You are not sick enough."

I smiled. He was right. I was fine and didn't need food prepared. You go from being an independent person to being mono-focused on personal health and recovery with people calling and asking to help. Then one day, you are near the end of your treatment and then the day comes when you don't need help.

———————— CHAPTER FOUR

Lesson 3
Life Back to Normal
Is a Life of Loneliness

W hen you are sick, a funny thing happens… friends and family make time for you. Your calls get answered immediately (no voicemail). I was amazed by this. Once my network of friends, family, and colleagues were informed about my condition, every text was answered immediately, and every call was physically answered. I never got voicemail. The first question everyone asked was, "Is everything okay? Do you need something?" This lasted throughout the journey.

My friends were just like me… busy with no time. However, they found time to be there for me. Then chemo was over. This was supposed to be a joyous day!!! That last day at the infusion center, I brought in doughnuts, orange juice and champagne to celebrate with my nurses whom had been there through the journey. This was my last visit and the center was busy. There were other patients who were sick and patients who were there for the first time. I don't want to say no one cared but I was not the highest priority. I was fine. I had completed my treatment and was CANCER FREE! The nurses played the song I chose as my mantra, Gloria Gaynor's "I Will Survive" (1979), but no one enjoyed the snacks. Even my chemo buddy for that last session was working and had no

23

celebration planned afterwards. Suffice it to say this last treatment was anti-climactic.

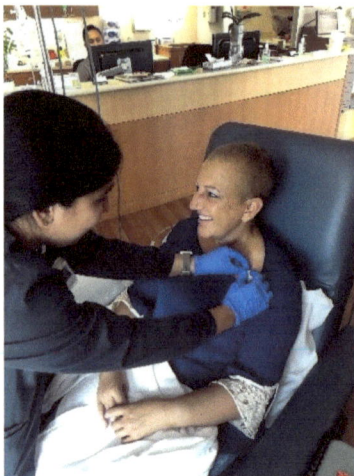

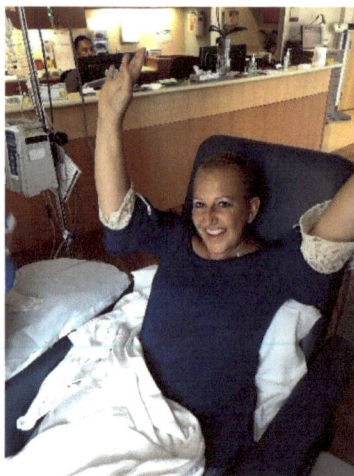

When I got home from my last treatment, I did have texts and messages from folks congratulating me. Then something happened. I didn't need help anymore. I was cancer-free and was finished with treatment. It was a bit of a sad day for me. For 5 months, I had rides to chemo. These were dedicated times with friends. Times where I got conversation and got to hear about their lives. I really did look forward to time with my friends. Then they stopped.

The first non-chemo Friday, I was happy and scheduled a massage. A real spa day! As I returned to a more normal work schedule, Fridays became a lonely day. During the cancer journey, I took every Friday off work for treatment. I had made a personal decision that I would continue not working Fridays. I would instead plan FUN things or schedule real spa treatments on Fridays. I was reprogramming my Fridays as a blessed gift of time to myself for all the times I worked late nights on Fridays just to get through the items on my desk. Fridays were now my time. But Fridays were now lonely.

24

Post-treatment, instead of knowing I was seeing a friend first thing in the morning on Friday, I now went to bed Thursday nights hoping I would get to see a friend (just one) the next day. I would try to schedule lunches or coffees for these Fridays. Or heck, I had the day off... let's go do something FUN!

I was hit with the same response, "I am sorry. I have to work."

"I am sorry. We are too busy... maybe next month?"

"I am sorry..."

"I am sorry" had become my worst nightmare. I felt blessed that I didn't get the "I am sorry" response when I was going through treatment, but sad that my friends returned to their lives. Meeting up was no longer a priority since I was healthy and didn't need anything. What they didn't understand was that I still needed them.

Post-treatment was literally like hitting a brick wall at 100 miles an hour. One day everyone was there for you. Then the day you are finished, everyone goes back to their lives. I don't know what I expected. I guess I finally realized that I loved spending time with my friends. I loved the backyard get-togethers with my neighbors. I loved the coffees, the lunches, the car rides where we just talked, and I got to laugh. I loved laughing with my friends.

I have been told that this phenomenon is normal. Life was getting back to normal. The old normal...not the new normal. I need to apologize to my friends for getting upset at them. I need them to know that I want the NEW normal. I want to spend time with them and do fun things. I declared 2018 the Year of Adventure and that is a year I will not spend alone. I just may now have to force folks to meet up with me. I may have to insist my friends carve out time. That is my gift back to my friends. The gift of reminding them that you don't have to "wait until someone shakes up the snow globe" to enjoy life. You don't have to wait until you retire to have fun. You just don't have to wait... to live!

If you are going through a rough patch, and you are longing for your friends to be there for you... or heck, if you just miss your friends because everyone is busy, remember that it is so easy these days to get caught up in life. Don't take it personally. Instead, tell them in a nice way you need them. It does take being vulnerable and sharing that you are in a bad space to help your friends prioritize seeing you. On the flip side, if you have friends going through rough patches (no matter how big or small), be there for them. Remember, asking is difficult. Hearing "No, I don't have time" can be more difficult.

Listen to how that sounds, "Sorry. I don't have time to see you, I am busy."

What just went through your head? What thoughts crossed your mind? How did you feel hearing those words? Remember that feeling and maybe instead of saying, "I am sorry... No... I just don't have time," try "Are you flexible on the date or time? I am sure we can make something work soon!"

————————CHAPTER FIVE

Lesson 4
You Can't Really
Plan the Future

T his seems like a simple lesson and so obvious. You probably
wondered why I even took time to call it out separately. I
mean, geez, I got cancer and of course that wasn't planned. But this
lesson hit home in more ways than just that.

Growing up, I was constantly asked, "What are you going to be
when you grow up? Where are you going to go to college? What
are you going to major in?"

When I finally graduated and got that first job, the company I
worked for asked me to set goals. What was I going to accomplish
this year? That process never stopped.

To make matters worse, I moved up the ranks and became a project
manager. Always planning and predicting what would happen in
the future on these projects.

Then I got cancer and my world changed. Planning *is* important,
but sometimes letting go and giving life time to unfold naturally is a
good thing. Sometimes not being so calculated and planned allows
for new life experiences to occur.

I had my whole life planned out when I was 16. I did. Honest... read my high school yearbook. I was going to be a pediatrician, get married in my 20's and have two kids. In reflection, none of those things happened. I am an entrepreneur running a successful consulting firm. I am single (searching for Mr. Right), and I have no kids unless you count Bordeaux my cat.

I took the planning thing a bit too far. I wasn't just planning a direction. I had every detail planned out. As I moved into adulthood that planning down to the lowest detail continued. It went further to planning out my days by the minute. (Did you read the first paragraph explaining the day of my re-imaging?) I had every day programmed. Wake up at 6:00am. Check my financial investments. Work... eat... sleep... repeat.

By planning every minute, I couldn't see that my life was unfolding in a negative direction. I couldn't see my life was unfolding in a way that was secluding me from family and friends. I was too busy to go to dinner parties. I was too busy (or tired) to play tennis. Oh gosh, don't even mention golf. That takes five to six hours and can kill a day! See how I described that? *Kill a day...* golf is FUN and what a blessing to have a full day to play and relax on the course. However, I was busy (just look at my calendar), and I was successful. It had been three to four years since I picked up my tennis racket. It was three years since I played golf. (Except for that one time my neighbor Adam took me out on the Country Club course... I couldn't pass up that once-in-a-life time opportunity!) It had been 10-12 years since I took a vacation (non-work related and more than just a long weekend).

I was planned out for months. My plans were focused around long work days and networking for business. I didn't know any better. Everyone was doing it! (Sounds like a drug prevention commercial). Everyone WAS doing it. All my friends were busy with work, kid sports, etc.

28

My Dad retired at 72 not because he wanted to, but because he was forced to due to health issues. My Dad and Mom instilled hard work pays off. Save… save… save. Work… work… work. My parents still ask me if I am working today when they call. They never ask, "What do you have planned this weekend? What fun is in your schedule?"

I am learning (and it isn't easy) that you don't have to be programmed every minute of every day. It is okay to say, "You know, I have nothing planned." This doesn't mean you are not living. It just means you are available for the unexpected! This doesn't mean you are not productive or that you are not successful because you have not scheduled every minute of the work week. It means that you might actually have time to decompress. That you can meditate or just sit and be one with your surroundings.

I really had planned to be married by age 22. Man, did I get that one wrong. I came close a few times (three actually) but the relationships just were not right for marriage. Later, I even put dating on hold as I didn't really have time. I found myself going out on dates and having debates with myself on if the person was worth my time. Did I enjoy their company more than I enjoyed my work? WHAT? After reading that sentence, I must sound like a crazy person, but it was true. Was the date worth my time? Remember, I am a busy person!

I am grateful for the lesson *You Can't Really Plan the Future*. There really is so much that is outside our control. God has the reigns. During my journey, I reconnected with my church. I have been attending my first ever bible study. Me? In bible study? Just nine months ago, I was only going to church a few times a year. Now, I am going on a non-Sunday to learn more about God. During one of the classes, the teacher said, "If you want to make God laugh, tell him your plan."

I smiled. Which one? Which plan should I tell him first? I smiled because I had plans for everything. And when I was fighting cancer, none of my plans were important. I didn't look at any of them. Oh yes, my plans are documented and updated annually. I told you, I had mastered the art of planning! What I learned (and still am learning) is that plans are okay, but don't be so focused on the plan that you miss living your life. I am finally AWAKE and ALIVE at 47 (now 48). I want to run my toes in the sand and let my mind wander free… free of thoughts. It is okay to breathe. Experience today the way it was intended... eyes and mind open to whatever unfolds. I have been practicing. When I am present in the moment (really present) things happen; things I would have missed before.

I was taking my yoga class when a new student stopped and talked to me. She said, "I think you should check out the Danville Yoga and Wellness Studio." She even gave me the class I needed to check out. This was odd. Normally, I would be so busy and not talk to anyone. I would go to class and leave immediately afterwards. But just by being open and saying, "Hi," I got a great tip for a new class to try. Coincidentally, I had just mentioned to a friend that I needed to find a class that was similar but cheaper as I needed to cut back on my spending. This new class was a fraction of the cost and was pay as you go. PERFECT!

Not being so programmed or scheduled has allowed me to be more open to just talking to people. I enjoy my surroundings and don't feel rushed. In the past, I took time to have coffee with friends. However, if you asked me what we talked about, I couldn't tell you. My thoughts were consuming my head and I don't think I really heard the conversation.

Now, for the first time, I am at peace and don't feel like my schedule has taken over my life. I was at lunch this past Wednesday with my friend Tracy (with a Y) and her Mom Donna.

Tracy just beat breast cancer for the second time! We ate lunch and then we had coffee. Then the idea came up to get ice cream. Since I was the one driving, they both stared at me to see what I thought. I found myself saying, "I don't have to be anywhere. We can do whatever. I am in!"

I am going to save that phrase and put in as my screen saver. I need to remember to not let my schedule get crazy busy. I need to allow myself time with friends and to not be rushed when I am with friends. I need to be present... present in the moment as you never know what you can learn or who you may run into!

CHAPTER 6

Lesson 5
Learning to be
Okay with Me

T his was a tough lesson. The teachings kept coming. They started with the first surgery and continued. They continue, and I am two months post chemotherapy and two weeks post reconstructive surgery.

So, you get diagnosed with breast cancer. From that moment on, you can forget modesty. To every person you tell this to, you are essentially sharing that *your breasts* have cancer, and something is going to happen.

You, as the patient, typically get to decide the surgical approach. I was fortunate to be in this category. I opted to pick the surgical approach with the lowest probability of reoccurrence. Decision number one done!

So, now I am sharing with friends, family, and heck, work colleagues and clients that I need to go in for a double mastectomy. I am sharing details on a personal level. People genuinely cared and wanted to know and offer support. In a lot of cases, people knew someone else who had gone through similar situations and offered to share those stories. However, you do realize I was a private person until now? Now, I am talking about removing my breasts as if I were going in to have a wart cut off.

Now, fast forward post-surgery. I now have no breasts. Just a divot where they used to be located.

I never really put a lot of my identity in my breasts. I mean, I thought more highly of my intellect and personality. Mind you, that didn't mean I didn't want to feel feminine. Having no breasts was very emasculating. I found myself wearing bulky shirts to camouflage. Now, with today's medical advancements, they inserted chest expanders (empty breast implants that can be filled or expanded). These serve as temporary placeholders until the patient can have reconstruction surgery. After the first month of recovery, I started having the expanders filled. It helped me feel more feminine. I decided to have fun with this. I decided to get them filled to the max. This took pretty much five months of fill-up visits. I said, "Let's try before I buy." When else can I get to try out different breast sizes? The first humbling moment averted. I came to peace with this quickly.

Just a month and a half after surgery, I started chemotherapy. The regiment was intense. I was told my hair (all hair) would start falling out 21 days after that first treatment and to be prepared. What does that mean? How does one prepare for hair fallout? Really? So, I researched. They said to maybe get a pre-chemo short haircut. My hair was long. So, going to a shorter cut might be good. Consider it done! I was off to the hairdresser.

Then, I got to thinking. They said all hair was going to fall out. That meant eye lashes and eye brows. For eye lashes, they have falsies I could turn to. For eye brows, I never was a big make up person. So, penciling scared me. With nothing there to even guide me, how could I ensure they were even? I decided to get my first tattoo! I got my eye brows tattooed. It was the best move ever. Even when I was so sick, I at least was able to wake up, look in the mirror, and feel somewhat like Traci.

34

It was two weeks until my first chemo treatment, and I was freaking out. Waiting was the worst. Then I was talking with colleagues and they said, "Are you going to try Cold Capping or are you going to try not having to shampoo for a few months?"

I thought, "What? What is Cold Capping?" Apparently, it is a process that attempts to save your hair during chemo treatment. Essentially, you wear a cap that keeps your scalp cold. The theory is the coldness narrows the blood vessels beneath the skin reducing the amount of chemotherapy medicine affecting your hair follicles. (Search for an article entitled "Cold Caps and Scalp Cooling Systems" February 23, 2018 at www.BreastCancer.org for more information.)

OH MY GOSH. Why am I just finding out about this now? Why hasn't anyone (doctors, nurses etc.) mentioned this?

Well, I tried Cold Capping. It is a very laborious process. It takes a lot of time and ideally two people to administer the caps. The caps must be changed frequently (approximately every 20-25 minutes). So, if you have an hour drive to chemo, you would have to pull over and change the caps on the side of the road. After all the reading and researching, I said, "I WANT THIS!" I really didn't want to lose my hair. My hair was my identity. I loved my hair.

I signed up for Cold Capping. To ensure I got the right and best system, I signed up with both vendors which I found available on-line. My parents were the ones taking me to my first chemo appointment. In preparation, we downloaded the video and printed the training materials. We even decided to hire a trainer to assist with the first session. Man, it was a tough! I handled the cold, but the chemo makes you sick. I couldn't handle throwing up and trying to change caps in-between. It was rough, but I was determined.

The next challenge. I now had to ask friends to not only take me to chemo but to agree to learn this process. This required that they had to stay with me much longer as the cold had to be applied in advance and well after the chemo treatment. Travis and Valerie were up next for the second chemo treatment. Both were willing to learn and administer the capping. They did a great job!!!

Then it started. Twenty-seven days after the first chemo treatment, my hair started to fall out in large clumps - even with Cold Capping. Not just like one clump a day. I would be sitting at my desk responding to email, and then I'd look down. I had a coat of hair gathering on my chest. When I touched my hair, another clump would fall out. At the end of one day, I had a waste basket full of hair. I uncontrollably cried. Really Cancer?!?! I am doing everything I can to save this hair, and you are going to still take it. You took my boobs. Isn't that enough? Apparently not. I stopped Cold Capping. It was expensive, and now I was defeated. Cancer was winning.

I immediately called a few close friends and said, "Okay. We need to go wig shopping ASAP." I couldn't go bald without a wig. I mean, I was still trying to run my business and appear normal out in public. Without hair, everyone would know I was undergoing treatment. I didn't want folks to pity me or treat me differently. I had my hair shaved military short and started wearing Wanda my Wig. It was humbling meeting friends without the wig. One just can't wear it all the time. And when folks came over to visit, sometimes I just felt sick, tired and just lucky to be sitting up right. So, I warned them. Difficult and humbling.

36

The hardest time was showing my baldness to Travis. This was someone I loved and someone I respected. We had so much chemistry in the past between us. I feared it would change his viewpoint of me. I still, for some reason, needed his approval. Odd, I know. But he touched my life in a positive way and our only disagreement used to be on the seriousness of our relationship. We agreed we were great together, but he was hard to pin down for any length of time. For some reason, I still needed him to validate me as a woman. I didn't have any desire to get back together. (Please, I have bigger things on my mind like kicking Cancer's ass!!) But I needed hugs, and I needed validation that I was still beautiful.

I was over at his house one afternoon helping him with work. Of course, I had on the wig and put on some makeup. I was out in public and needed to feel normal. We talked, and I shared what it was like going bald. He mentioned he could relate but then added his hair won't grow back. We both laughed. In support, he offered to shave his head, so we would be bald together. Such a nice gesture that made me realize that he still cared for me as a good friend. I was comforted. I took off my wig. I looked down and just cried. He knew that was a big step and just offered very supportive words. A moving moment for me.

For those of you that know me, you know I am not one to feel sorry for myself… at least not for very long. So, I decided after that day that I needed to look at this differently. I needed to say, "TAKE MY HAIR... ALL OF IT!!! Chemo kill any bad news cells!!!" I don't want bad or unhealthy cells. This is a time for my body to rebirth itself. It is a time for healthy cells, healthy hair, etc. to have a chance to be reborn.

For the next three to four months, I watched as every hair on my head fell out. I took pictures weekly with my phone. I sat on the couch and took photos of the back of my head. Any new hair??? I took photos of the top of my head. Any new hair? Any stubble? I compared the weekly photos.

In the meantime, I would look in the mirror and say, "Hello, Stunt Double. I am not sure what you did with Traci, but I am sure you are only here temporarily until she can return."

Calling the person in the mirror my Stunt Double made it easier. It made it feel temporary; like how stunt doubles stand in during the tough and rough scenes and the real actor appears when the rough stuff is over. That is how I pictured it. My stunt double was standing in until the rough stuff was over.

You know, the things I went through with chemo are not unlike everyday life. When are we ever really happy with our appearance? I remember for so many years, I kept saying if I could only just lose ten more pounds. If only my hair was just a bit blonder... or a bit less curly. Now I found, I got so happy when I stopped losing weight and even happier when I had actual stubble on my head. It is different to say, "Hey. I have two, count them two, eye lashes left." Compare this to, "Hey. I have two new eyelashes. Look at them!!!"

So, I waited... sometimes patiently... sometimes not so patiently... for the new and improved Traci to arrive. Well, I would have just been happy with any Traci. I just wanted to start feeling normal.

Why are we conditioned to look for flaws in ourselves? We are hit with magazine and TV ads focused on losing weight, using this wrinkle reducer, getting rid of fat without exercise, or hey, to exercise more!

During this journey I just had to be okay with me. The me that showed up today; whatever that looked like. Being on chemo was the first time since I was 16 that I put my diet books away. It was the first time I ate whatever I wanted - this included grilled cheese, french toast, chicken noodle casserole, etc. I don't think I ate a vegetable for nine months! (Not that I recommend that.)

My point is, I took the focus on what I should be doing (dieting and counting calories) and focused on just how I felt. I found time to just do normal skin care (cleanse, moisturize, repeat). Friends kept saying, "Your skin looks great!" Hmm... well, I am having the time to wash my face and use a good moisturizer. Crazy. In life's hustle and bustle during my life pre-cancer, I put myself last. Normal good hygiene was only if I had time or wasn't too tired. Dieting was 24x7, and all it did was left me upset. I always cheated since I was always hungry!

Being upset and stressed was my justification to winding down the day with wine. I mean, we all do it right? Life is stressful - wine helps! During treatment, I was too sick to drink and had to find other beverages to end the day; beverages that soothed the tummy. I was introduced to Ginger Tea. OH MY GOSH - a game changer.

During this whole process, I just had to get back-to-basics. Back to just being good with me - whatever me looked back in the mirror. A hard thing to do for anyone. Can you say you like the person staring back at you in the mirror? If not, why? Do you need to wait for a life changing event to make changes, or is there something you can do today to be more loving to the person in the mirror? So, you are carrying a few extra pounds. What if you didn't stress over that? What if you just focused on being more active and doing things that made you smile? Sometimes, just focusing on being happy with you has a side effect where you stop using food as a crutch. Maybe... it is different for everyone. I now say, "I love you," to the person in the mirror. "You look fabulous!"

No, my hair is not fully grown back. I am still missing eye lashes, and since it is winter, I am a bit washed-out looking. But you know,

I do *Love Myself.* I am grateful for every day I am alive and breathing!

CHAPTER 7

Lesson 6
Fake It Until
You Believe It

When you are going through health issues, it is common for people to ask you, "So, how are you doing? How are you feeling? Do you need anything?" The reality is you feel terrible and crappy. You wish this nightmare would be over. Sometimes you are angry at God. Sometimes you are sad. Sometimes you just don't have any ounce of energy left to feel anything.

I decided Cancer took a lot from me already, and it wasn't going to take away my spirit. How are you? A typical response to that question would be, "Fine. Thank you for asking." Or maybe, "Not so good today."

Instead, I decided to be bold and respond with, "Fabulous! I feel Fabulous!"

The looks I would get in return were interesting. "Wait, you just had chemo. How can you be fabulous? Mediocre maybe but Fabulous?"

"Yes. I FEEL FABULOUS!"

Mind you, today fabulous may just mean I wasn't on the couch all day not able to move. Or I was fabulous because all my food stayed down. Or wait, it may be that I could even eat today. *Fabulous* was my state of mind.

I can remember my visits with my oncologist. You must meet with them every few weeks during treatment. The doctor asked, "So, how are you today?"

I responded, "I am Fabulous. Thank you for asking."

She said, "What? You are going through cancer treatment and you are Fabulous?"

I smiled. "Oh. You wanted to know if I am experiencing any side-effects? Now, Doc that is a totally different question." I would continue by sharing the side-effects for that 2-week period. None of which were fun, but side effects didn't have to impede my state of mind. My body was a mess. (I smile when I type that sentence. A mess was an understatement.) Again, I decided to treat this like the old me is dying and a new me is emerging. I AM FABULOUS! I CAN'T WAIT!!! A new Traci is coming soon, and I can't wait to meet her! I love this stunt double, but I am ready for Traci to appear.

You know, a person's state of mind is interesting. I really do think I faked it until I believed it. I mean, I didn't really feel fabulous, but fabulous was the word I chose to express how I felt. Not good... not okay... I felt FABULOUS! I found that after responding this way, I started to smile more. I started to hold my head up a bit higher. I remember taking time every morning (some days 30 minutes some days 2 hours) to get cleaned up and put on makeup. Yes, every day. I had nowhere to be, but I felt clean and good.

I also found my friends felt relieved to get a "Fabulous" response. What I mean is, when you ask someone who is sick how they feel, you have no idea what the response will be. It is an open slate for the sick person to respond. Now, don't get me wrong. People genuinely care but remember people can't really do anything to make the situation better. They can only listen and say, "I am sorry."

If I would have responded with, "Oh let me tell you how bad it is...," my friends would have empathized, but they would start to look at me differently. They would start to pity me and (depending on how gruesome the stories I shared with them) they would be deterred from asking me in the future how I felt.

If the last thing I heard back from my friends was, "I am sorry," I would start to agree with them. Yes. It is sorry that I must go through this. I am a sorry mess!!! I just couldn't go there. I chose to BE FABULOUS!

When I checked in at my chemotherapy appointments, I would say, "Hi. I am here for my Spa Appointment."

The nurses would just laugh, smile and say, "Oh Miss Traci."

I would then say, "I would like a room with a view please." All infusion chairs had a window, but I tried to make this more fun. I brought magazines and fuzzy slippers. I really wanted to turn this negative event into something where I could look forward to it. In a weird way, I did look forward to it. The nurses were friendly. We would joke around. On certain days, the Infusion Center even had a massage therapist who would come around and do neck, shoulder or calf massages for you. It was quite nice. I loved doughnut day!

Now, I hated Thursday nights. That was the night before chemo. Most Thursdays, I tried to keep it together. Be strong. You can do this... only X more treatments! But on some Thursdays, I couldn't pull it together. Travis worked nights, so I leaned on him for support. He always knew what to say or what to respond. I would then wake up Friday and say, "Okay stunt double... Let's do this!"

43

I also found comfort by leaning on God. At times, I was angry. "Really, God? I need to go through this? Wasn't I a good person?"

Then I took a step back. After surgery and all the tests, I had Stage Two breast cancer. It was estrogen feeding and aggressive, but it was NOT in the lymph nodes. This was great news! So, I never felt I was going to die. I don't feel this was a death sentence at all. I really believe it was a wakeup call.

Pre-cancer, I was focused on work and clients and how I could make more money and buy bigger things. I had friends, but there was never time for them. Well, to be honest, they were going through the same craziness called life and had no time for me either. Time was scarce.

Now, during treatment and recovery, all I had was time. A lot of it. A lot of time alone. I did wonder why I needed more time alone (chuckling to myself). Apparently, there was a lesson I needed to learn.

What I took away from this is my life is a blessing. Each day is a gift. How I choose to spend my day and how I choose to feel are all in my control. I realized that the crazy life I had pre-cancer was the life I created. No one was to blame but myself. Life was playing out just like I orchestrated. Work, work, work, work, and more work. Fun? Only if there's time and if there was no work to do. Better yet, could I combine work with fun?

During recovery, I found that being home all day was depressing. I needed friends and planned outings to stay positive. So, I worked hard to schedule visits (whether in my house or out), but always with friends. With me not working very much during this time, we had to talk about non-work topics. This was challenging. What did I have to share that was not work? Hmm... right now, just my health issues, but that was depressing. I really had to dig to find

44

topics of conversation. I made a mental note to remember that situation. I needed to remember that when I felt better, I needed to schedule fun events. I wanted to be able to talk about more than just work and health. The responses needed to be about what experiences I was living!

Six weeks after my last chemotherapy treatment, I went to Squaw Valley and took a ski lesson. Yes. I FELT FABULOUS! Now mind you, I couldn't make it through the whole lesson as my body was still weakened from chemo. I went back to the hotel and slept for 14 hours, but I did it! I skied! I DID FEEL FABULOUS! I also felt well accomplished.

Having a positive attitude can be catchy and addicting… just like a bad attitude can be additive. I chose to stay positive. I love that *Monty Python* movie quote, "It's only a flesh wound...get back here you sissy!!!" (*Monty Python and the Holy Grail*, 1975)

What do you do when you are down and out? Do you wade in the realms of self-pity? If so, that is okay. It is normal. But how long do you stay there? What if you picked different responses to the phrases, "How do you feel today?" or "How are you?" How can you fake until you believe it?

CHAPTER EIGHT

Lesson 7
You Can't
Have It All Right Now

I am finished with treatment and CANCER FREE! As I mentioned earlier in the book, I declared 2018 the "Year of My Greatest Adventures and Grandest Dreams" (Oprah Winfrey, *O, The Oprah Magazine*, January 2017). Each passing day, I had increasingly more energy. Keep in mind that having more energy just meant I didn't need naps but was still in bed by 8pm (laugh out loud). With no doctor appointments and no treatment sessions, I wanted to live full out and I wanted to live FULL OUT NOW! I didn't want God to think I wasn't grateful. I didn't want to waste any time; not even a minute!

If I was awake, I wanted to ensure I was living purposefully. I wanted to ensure I wasn't falling back into my habits of working 24x7. I wanted to play. I wanted to laugh. More importantly, I wanted to love. To love my family, to love my friends... just to love and be loved. I wanted the first day of the rest of my life to start now!

I started planning outings. I planned a learn-to-ski weekend six weeks post chemo. I did it but was exhausted for days afterwards! I then planned a wild New Year's Eve outing which was seven days post reconstruction surgery and eight weeks post chemotherapy.

Three days later, I got the flu and was out of commission and on the couch sleeping a lot. It took ten days to fully recover. With each activity came a consequence; usually sleeping for days.

What I realized was I have the rest of my life! I don't have to live it all in one weekend. Ha! I should plan to be out with friends and plan one big adventure monthly. The key was to just not be okay with being on the couch or working 24x7. Take in God's creations and really absorb the beauty that is just all around us.

I realized post recovery that living was like running a half marathon. (I chose this analogy because I have actually run two half marathons thanks to my friend Amanda.) When you decide to run, you don't sign up and just show up the day of the event. Nor do you show up and start running at full force. You pace yourself to reserve the body fuel for the duration of the event. Training itself takes planning and preparation. First, you find an event and you register. Then you determine what shape

you are in and how much training you will need. You then back into the start date to figure out when you should start your training. You train three times a week (not every day) for ten weeks.

48

Living is much the same. You don't have to schedule things every day (or even 2 days in a row). You space out the training (aka Adventures). This allows for less injury and or interruption to training. It also minimizes pain. In Adventureland, it spaces out the enjoyment and happiness. If you got all your travels for the year completed in the first week of January, what would you have to look forward to? I found what sustained me during the low points of treatment was having something to look forward to.

Part of living is also remembering that Relaxing and Resting is part of living. I didn't want to go from being over-scheduled with work to now being over-scheduled with just anything. Even if that anything is FUN. The key is being okay. If you start from a place of being okay, you don't get polarized with those feelings of missing out. You instead know that you are doing what you should be doing at this very moment. Like right now, I am writing this chapter while sitting outside. I just glanced up and spent five minutes just watching the hummingbirds play and chase each other. Counting blessings, even the small ones, is what life is all about. It is about enjoying your surroundings, people, places and things. The over used phrase says it all "Take time to smell the roses."

Are you moving too fast? Are you over-scheduled and find yourself with no time? Whether you are over-scheduled with work or with too many adventures, remember Life is about the Journey. It is about that "second lane of a two-way street." Who or what is passing you by on the other side? What friends have you neglected? What friendships are just one sided and could use attention?

What if you slowed down and took time to be with friends and grow or deepen those friendships? What if you took time to just be with you and your thoughts? Do your thoughts scare you? Mine scare me as they are often about what I should be doing. I am trying to change that. So, don't beat yourself up if it takes a while to change your habits.

Life is not a marathon… it isn't lived in one day. It is about experiences and love. Live for today and don't worry about what tomorrow may or may not bring. I only ask you to "Just don't wait for your snow globe to be shaken…"

A Letter to My Friends

December 10, 2017

Every year I pick a theme; kind of like a mantra.

> 2015 was the year of Joy.
> 2016 was the year of Blessings.
> 2017 The Year of Love!

The year recapped…

2017 started off much like every year. January was spent recuperating from the holidays… treadmill, diet, and sleep. I was on target to really explode in my business. TEngle Consulting Group turned 8 this year. Then came March....

On March 21st, I was diagnosed with Breast Cancer. It was a day I will never forget. It was one of those events that stops your life dead in its tracks and forces you to focus and reprioritize.

I was told on a Tuesday. By that Friday, I had completed three doctor appointments and a boat load of tests including X-rays, MRIs blood work and DNA testing. All of this needed to determine the severity and to help me determine my course of action. It's funny how just one week ago, work and corporate meetings were filling my day. Now, doctor appointments consumed my time. Trust me, the decisions I had to make were not ones I would want my biggest enemy to have to make. My only objective at that moment was GET IT OUT ASAP!!!! And the surgical option had to be the one that

gave me the greatest odds for full recovery with ZERO recurrence.
I chose the most aggressive surgical procedure.

I was blessed that my family was there for me. They flew out and
stayed. They stayed until I fully recovered from surgery. Mom and
Dad took care of me. My sister Chris flew out and helped as well.
Chris and Dad got my back yard ready for spring and summer.
They knew how I love to sit out back and watch the hummingbirds.
So, they worked to make it perfect! Mom held down the fort on the
inside and made all my favorite meals - chicken noodle casserole,
stuffed peppers and grilled cheese. In addition, I am blessed to have
such great friends. I was surrounded by LOVE! It was because of
that LOVE that I felt I was able to get through this horrific journey
with all the strength and positivity that I could muster.

Surgery went well. I was just feeling normal when the final
pathology test results came in. The cancer was Stage I at time of
diagnosis. It was now Stage II (meaning it grew). There are
different types of cancer cells. They measure how aggressively the
cells divide (meaning bad news). I had the worst type - aggressive.
This meant I would need chemotherapy. I would not need radiation.

Diagnosis - March 21, surgery - April 20th, Chemo - started June 8th.
I finished October 20! Final Reconstruction was scheduled for
December 22.

Mom and Dad flew back out to take me to my first chemo session.
I know how tough that day was for me; fear of that poison flowing
through my veins and what side effects were going to hit. I cannot
imagine what my parents went through that day. Watching a child
go through chemo has got to be one of the most trying days in one's

life. Once again, the love just flowed in. I was blessed to have rides to every chemo session. Chemo was weekly. At times, there were two chemo buddies! Mom, of course, left a freezer full of food but friends added to that. I had homemade soups, Jell-O and casseroles. Chemo is chemo. I will spare you the details and side-effects. All I will share is that it is very humbling. You look in the mirror and don't recognize the person staring back at you. I called that person my stunt double.

One-month post chemo, I am still followed around by my stunt double. I long for the day I can do a hair-flip (LOL) or the day my eye-lashes are back.

I decided Cancer took enough. It was not going to take my spirit. I chose the day I was diagnosed (well, maybe a week or so later after the shock and panic attacks subsided). I chose to LIVE. To LIVE FULL OUT. I wake up and just breath the fresh air and admire this glorious land we live in. I chose to no longer take my friends and family for granted. I chose to honor my body (whatever it looks like). I am deciding to Play, Laugh and Love more.

A Playful Moment
The only chance in my life when I can recreate a baby photo!

The theme photo for this Christmas letter is me learning to ski this December 9th - literally less than two months post chemo! Maybe a bit too soon to be fully back to normal energy and fitness level, BUT why wait to LIVE? Live today!!

Tomorrow the phone could ring, and your world could be turned upside down!

2018 is themed the "Year of my Greatest Adventures and Grandest Dreams" (Oprah Winfrey, *O, The Oprah Magazine*, January 2017).

I am counting on my friends and family to join me in these adventures. May God bless you and watch over you. May YOUR grandest dreams come true!

Traci

Acknowledgements

I am very blessed to have beat cancer. The journey is one I will never forget. There are over 100 people involved in my support and care - family, friends, colleagues, doctors, nurses and strangers. This book is for you. This book is for you to know how positively you impacted my life and enabled me to fight when I had no strength. This book is for those who have never known me. Maybe someone or something has "shaken up your snow globe." Maybe you need to know you are not alone and that what you are experiencing is normal. Maybe something in this book resonates and gives you hope to fight just one more day! Life is a journey, not a destination. It is the experiences and people on the journey that make us who we are today.

I want to specifically call out my parents. I can't even image what it is like to have your child tell you they have cancer. We, as children, expect to take care of our parents as years go by and not the other way around. Mom... Dad... knowing that you *had my back,* reduced my fears and allowed me to just focus on my health. There are no words that adequately describe my gratefulness. Humbly, I say, "THANK YOU!!"

www.ingramcontent.com/pod-product-compliance
Lightning Source LLC
Chambersburg PA
CBHW041530090426

42738CB00035B/23